Dear Parent:

Buckle up! You are about to join your child on a very exciting journey. The destination? Independent reading!

Road to Reading will help you and your child get there. The program offers books at five levels, or Miles, that accompany children from their first attempts at reading to successfully reading on their own. Each Mile is paved with engaging stories and delightful artwork.

Getting Started

For children who know the alphabet and are eager to begin reading

• easy words • fun rhythms • big type • picture clues

Reading With Help

For children who recognize some words and sound out others with help

• short sentences • pattern stories • simple plotlines

Reading On Your Own

For children who are ready to read easy stories by themselves

• longer sentences • more complex plotlines • easy dialogue

First Chapter Books

For children who want to take the plunge into chapter books

• bite-size chapters • short paragraphs • full-color art

Chapter Books

For children who are comfortable reading independently

• longer chapters • occasional black-and-white illustrations

There's no need to hurry through the Miles. Road to Reading is designed without age or grade levels. Children can progress at their own speed, developing confidence and pride in their reading ability no matter what their age or grade.

So sit back and enjoy the ride—every Mile of the way!

For Gerald Kruglik,
my sidekick, champion, and
match made in heaven
B.B.

For Avery Rose—
Queen of Spots
D.B.

Library of Congress Cataloging-in-Publication Data
Bottner, Barbara.
Marsha makes me sick / by Barbara Bottner ; illustrated by Denise Brunkus.
   p. cm. — (Road to reading. Mile 3)
Summary: Lulu's younger sister Marsha, who has the chicken pox, seems to be taking
all of their mother's time, and Lulu tries hard to get some attention of her own.
ISBN 0-307-26302-9
[1. Sisters—Fiction.   2. Mother and child—Fiction.   3. Chicken pox—Fiction.
4. Sick—Fiction.]   I. Brunkus, Denise, ill.   II. Title.
III. Series.
PZ7.B6586Mar 1998
[E]—dc21   98-5800
                                                               CIP
                                                               AC

A GOLDEN BOOK • New York
Golden Books Publishing Company, Inc. New York, New York 10106

ISBN: 0-307-26302-9

R MM

Marsha Makes Me Sick

by Barbara Bottner
illustrated by Denise Brunkus

"I feel horrible,"

Lulu said,

all alone in her room.

"Mom!" she called.

"There's nothing to do.

Will you play with me?"

"Lulu," her mom said.

"I'll be in as soon

as I take care of Marsha."

Marsha!

Lulu did not like

Marsha today.

Lulu did not like Marsha

any day.

Marsha cried.

Marsha slobbered.

Marsha could only say

ten words.

Everybody loved Marsha.

Lulu sang.

Lulu danced.

Lulu told jokes.

Lulu could write her name

in cursive.

Nobody loved Lulu.

"Marsha makes me sick,"

said Lulu.

She went to the window.

Outside the birds

were singing.

"Poor Lulu,

poor Lulu,"

they chirped.

Lulu wrapped herself

in a blanket.

She hobbled down the hallway.

Lulu went to Marsha's room.

"Marsha looks fine,"

said Lulu.

"I look like melted cheese."

"Loo-lah," said Marsha.

Marsha was so dumb.

She did not even know

how to say Lulu.

"Try to be a big girl

and go play by yourself,"

said Lulu's mom.

"Your poor sister is sick

with the chicken pox."

Lulu did her best death walk.

"Be nice to me," moaned Lulu.

"These are my last moments.

What about poor Lulu?"

Lulu looked like she was going

to fall over.

Lulu did fall over.

"Lulu, please!"

said her mom.

"I'm trying to get Marsha

to sleep.

Now be a good big sister

and be quiet!"

Lulu went into the den.

"Marsha makes me sick,"

she said.

The birds were still chirping,

"Poor Lulu. Poor Lulu."

Lulu plopped down

on the sofa.

She landed on

Marsha's teddy bear.

Marsha was always

leaving her toys

in dumb places.

She found the remote

under the pillow.

"You can watch TV

with me, Teddy,"

she said.

"You are my only friend today."

Lulu turned on the TV.

There was a movie on TV

about a monster.

It was a big scary monster

who was eating up people.

"Eeeek!" screamed Lulu.

"Mom! Help!

The monster is going

to eat me!"

"Lulu!" her mother called

from the kitchen.

"Stop being a baby!"

Lulu curled up

into a ball.

"If the monster gets me

you will all be sad,"

she said.

Lulu could see it now.

Her whole family

would go on TV.

Marsha would say,

"Lulu was the good one.

Lulu was the best big sister

in the world."

Her dad would say,

"Lulu was the smart one."

Her mom would say,

"She knew how to write cursive."

Lulu's mom came out

of the kitchen.

She was carrying

a bottle of milk for Marsha.

"Mom!" said Lulu.

"I am hungry!"

"Can you make yourself

a sandwich?" her mom asked.

"No," cried Lulu.

But her mom was already gone.

"I will have to make lunch for myself,"

said Lulu.

"Or I will starve."

She took out the milk.

She took out the bread and jam.

"Lunch for two, Teddy!"

she called.

She put everything

on a tray,

and took it into the den.

"Here you go, Teddy,"

said Lulu.

"Here's a sandwich for you."

Splat!

"You are messy, Teddy," said Lulu.

The monster movie

was getting very scary.

The monster was making

terrible noises.

"Aaahhh," the monster moaned.

Lulu covered her eyes
and tried to turn off
the TV.

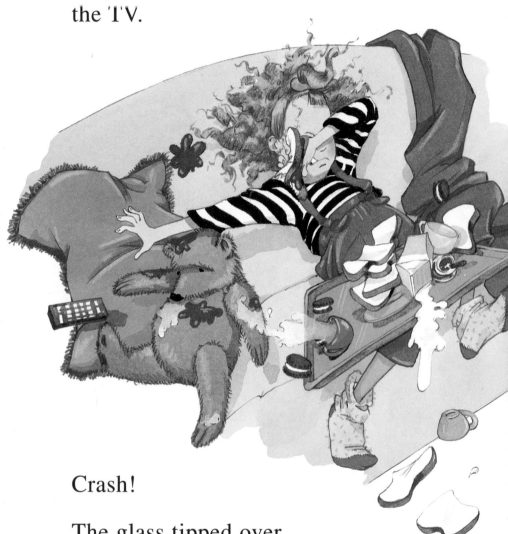

Crash!

The glass tipped over.

The milk spilled

on Teddy.

Lulu mopped up the milk

with the pillows.

Just then Lulu's mom came in.

"Lulu!" she cried.

"Look at this mess!

Jam all over the sofa!

Milk all over Teddy!

Crumbs all over the floor!"

Lulu's mom looked mad.

"It's all Marsha's fault," said Lulu.

"Lulu, poor Marsha is in bed

with the chicken pox,"

said her mom.

"Aaahhh!" cried the TV monster.

Lulu's mom turned off the TV.

"You should not be watching

these monster movies."

Lulu went down the hall

and peeked into

Marsha's room.

Lulu went over

to the crib.

Marsha looked bad.

She had big red spots

all over her.

"Aaahhh," Marsha cried,

just like the monster.

"Loo-loo," said Marsha.

"That's right!"

said Lulu.

"I am your big sister.

I will be a good big sister.

I will stay here with you."

Lulu sat down

and soon

she fell asleep.

41

"Lulu," said her mom softly.

Lulu woke up.

Her mother was

looking down at her.

"I'm trying to be

a good sister," said Lulu.

"You are a good sister,"

said her mom.

"But right now you are

a good sick sister."

Lulu looked down.

She had red spots

all over her.

She looked worse

than Marsha!

"Aaahhh!" cried Lulu.

"Into bed," her mother said.

Lulu's mom tucked the covers

around her.

"Poor Lulu," she said.

"You caught the chicken pox

from Marsha."

"Poor Lulu," said Lulu.

"I try to be a good sister.

But Marsha makes me sick!"